SUPER CITIES!

SEATTLE

by James Buckley Jr.

arcadia®
CHILDREN'S BOOKS

Published by Arcadia Children's Books
A Division of Arcadia Publishing
Charleston, SC
www.arcadiapublishing.com

Super Cities is a trademark of Arcadia Publishing, Inc.

First published 2021

Manufactured in the United States.

ISBN 978-1-4671-9849-3

Library of Congress Control Number: 2021943247

Notice: The information in this book is true and complete to the best of our knowledge. It is offered without guarantee on the part of the author or Arcadia Publishing. The author and Arcadia Publishing disclaim all liability in connection with the use of this book.

Produced by Shoreline Publishing Group LLC
Santa Barbara, California
Designer: Patty Kelley

Contents

WELCOME TO Seattle!

Look at a map of the United States. Now head north (up) and west (to the left). And you're there—the Pacific Northwest! You've reached the state of Washington. And that state's biggest city is Seattle!

Seattle is an amazing place. A giant troll lives there. There's a tower of guitars! You can ride the train of the future and see statues of the past. Visit islands, climb a needle, and duck! Watch out for flying fish! Don't worry—inside, we'll explain what all that means.

Seattle,
Washington

FAST FACTS
Seattle, Washington
POPULATION:
725,000
FOUNDED:
1851
NICKNAMES:
The Queen City
The Emerald City

When you visit Seattle, you'll see a lot of water. Seattle is almost entirely surrounded by water (see page 7). Some of it is salty like the ocean. Some of the water is fresh like a lake. Boaters, sailors, and fisherpeople find lots to do in Seattle. But all around the water and the city are beautiful tall mountains in almost every direction you look. Seattle is famous for its natural beauty and its creative people. Inside this book, we'll visit all those places and meet a lot of those people. **Let's go to Seattle!**

SEATTLE: Map It!

Most of the city of Seattle is on a long, thin piece of land. To the west is Puget Sound. Boats filled with fish and visitors travel down the Sound from the Pacific Ocean. Water taxis and ferries speed people—and their cars—to islands (and some people even live on boats!). To the east of Seattle is the huge Lake Washington. It's one of the biggest lakes in a city in the United States!

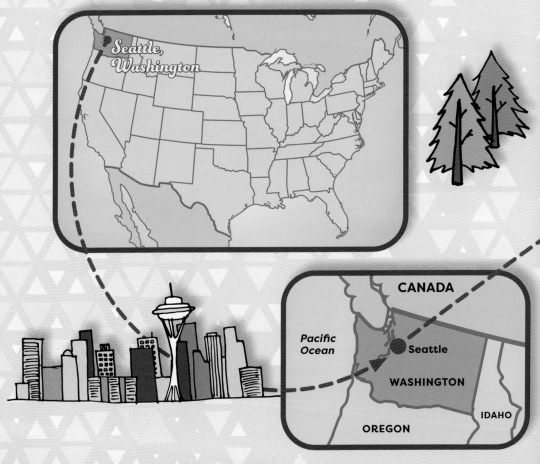

Seattle, Washington

CANADA

Pacific Ocean

Seattle

WASHINGTON

IDAHO

OREGON

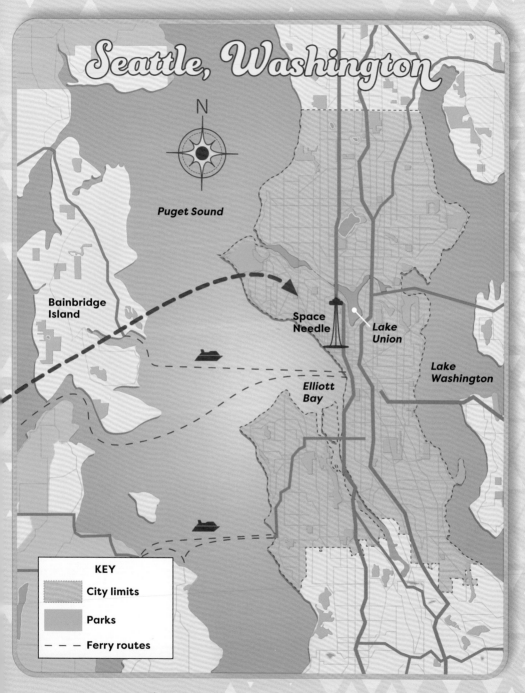

Seattle, Washington

Puget Sound

N

Bainbridge Island

Space Needle

Lake Union

Lake Washington

Elliott Bay

KEY

City limits

Parks

– – – Ferry routes

Set the Scene

Lake Washington is a great place to go fishing. Catch trout, bass, and sometimes salmon in the second largest lake in the state.

Seattle Center is packed with fun things to do. Museums, parks, fountains, restaurants, concerts— if you like it, you'll find it here!

It's a clear day—so Mount Rainier makes an appearance! The glacier-covered peak stands 14,411 feet high. It's a tough climb, but rugged hikers can usually make it all the way up! (Rainier is an active volcano, but don't worry: it last blew its top in 1894.)

Check out a forest trail on Bainbridge Island. British explorer George Vancouver landed here in 1792, but it was an American sailor who named the island for U.S. Navy hero Charles Bainbridge. Today, it's home to tons of great hiking and biking trails and a beautiful small town.

Find a great place to walk along Puget Sound's 1,300 miles of coastline. In this body of water, the salty ocean meets freshwater coming from the south.

SEATTLE
MEANS . . .

Believe it or not, Seattle was first called New York (sort of!). For thousands of years, the land around Seattle was home to the Suquamish and Duwamish people. White settlers arrived in the 1850s, and they built a small village. They named it for another famous city, New York. But they added a word from the Chinook language, another Native people of the area. So New York-Alki was born.

That name didn't last long. As the village grew, the white settlers chose a new name to honor the chief of the Native nations. He was called Chief Si'ahl in his people's language, Salish. It was also spelled Sealth. American settlers changed it to . . . Seattle! By 1852, the city had the name it uses today.

This bust of the chief looks over Pioneer Square.

This is a colored postcard of one of the only photos of the real Chief Si'ahl.

ONE BiG WHEEL!

It's 174 feet tall!

42 cars can hold eight people each.

When it opened in 2012, it was the biggest Ferris wheel on the West Coast.

A ride once around takes from 10 to 20 minutes.

The Seattle Great Wheel is a huge Ferris wheel on the Puget Sound waterfront. It rises high above Pier 57. Riders in the cars soar above the city to get great views in every direction. It's one of the biggest attractions in town, so here are some things you need to know!

One of the cars has a glass floor! Yikes!

When it's full, the wheel can hold 332 people.

For part of each ride, you are suspended over the water—that's a Ferris wheel first!

Colored LED lights on the wheel dazzle on summer weekend nights.

HISTORY: Early Days

People have been living around Puget Sound for more than 10,000 years. The Duwamish and Suquamish people built villages near the waters of the area. Many spoke the Salish language. This helped them communicate with each other. They also created beautiful baskets, beadwork, and boats, some of which can still be seen today. In 1850 the U.S. Government created the Donation Land Act which took the land away from the indigenous people and gave it to white settlers. Today, nearly all of their land, and much of the indigenous culture, in the area has been lost.

Tall, carved wooden poles are often seen around Seattle. However, they came from First Nations (Canada) people including Chinook, Tlingit, Haida, and others, not from the Suquamish people.

Native people found plenty of salmon to eat.

The Native people used all parts of nature. They weaved baskets from tree bark.

This photo is from the early 1900s. But it shows a style of canoe the Duwamish people have used for centuries.

British explorer George Vancouver sailed into upper Puget Sound in 1792. He didn't even stay long enough for a cup of Starbucks coffee!

1851: The 24 members of the Denny family were part of a long wagon train from their home in Indiana. They were among tens of thousands of white settlers who headed west into the land of Native Americans. In 1851, members of the Denny family arrived in Oregon.

Later that year, David Denny walked into Seattle on foot. He wrote to his brother, Arthur, about what he had found. The area had a wide area that could be a port for ships. The land was mostly flat and looked ready for farming. "Come at once!"

David Denny

Arthur Denny

November 13, 1851: Arthur and the rest of the Denny group arrived after sailing into Puget Sound. Over the next few years, they built homes and other buildings. They started farming. In 1905, the city put up this monument to the Denny family.

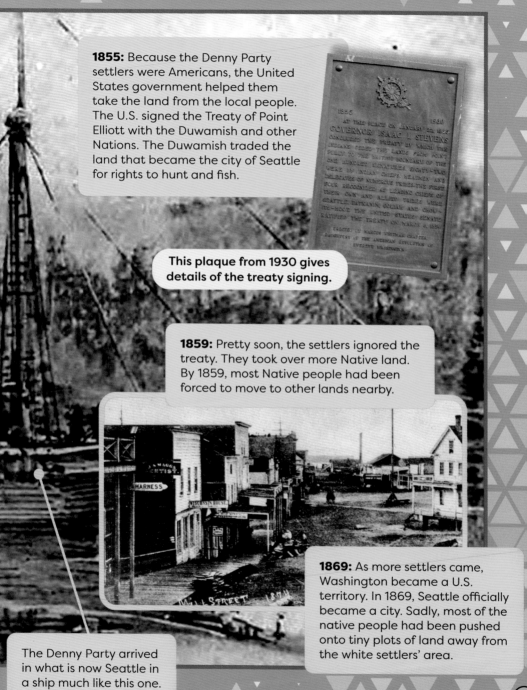

1855: Because the Denny Party settlers were Americans, the United States government helped them take the land from the local people. The U.S. signed the Treaty of Point Elliott with the Duwamish and other Nations. The Duwamish traded the land that became the city of Seattle for rights to hunt and fish.

This plaque from 1930 gives details of the treaty signing.

1859: Pretty soon, the settlers ignored the treaty. They took over more Native land. By 1859, most Native people had been forced to move to other lands nearby.

1869: As more settlers came, Washington became a U.S. territory. In 1869, Seattle officially became a city. Sadly, most of the native people had been pushed onto tiny plots of land away from the white settlers' area.

The Denny Party arrived in what is now Seattle in a ship much like this one.

1860s: People from China began arriving in Seattle. Not long after, Japanese workers started coming to get jobs in lumber mills in the nearby forests. Parts of Seattle soon became identified with these groups.

1883: We want the railroad! The Northern Pacific Railroad said it would stop at Tacoma, Washington. Tacoma is a city about thirty-three miles south of Seattle. No fair! Seattle citizens complained, and the railroad changed its mind. The first trains arrived in Seattle in 1883!

1889: A huge fire destroyed hundreds of wooden buildings in town. But Seattle rebuilt quickly. Newer buildings (right) were made of stone and brick. During the rebuilding, a large part of the old city was buried underground (page 37!).

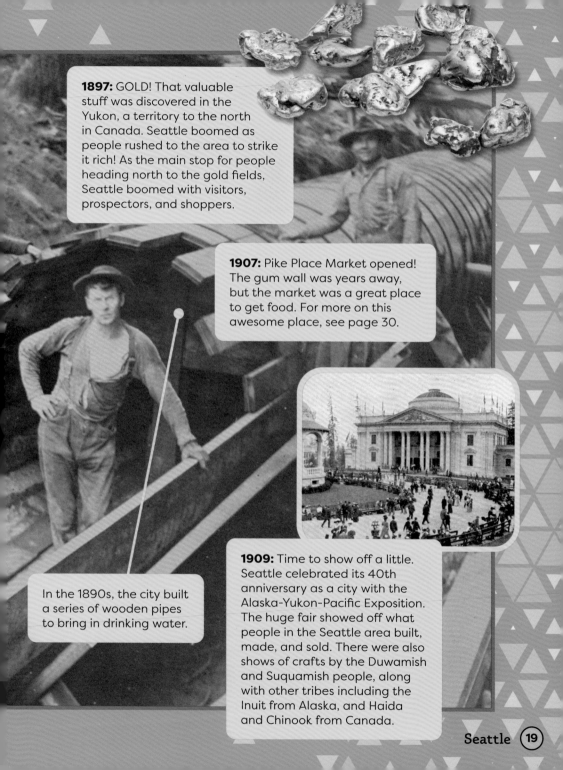

1897: GOLD! That valuable stuff was discovered in the Yukon, a territory to the north in Canada. Seattle boomed as people rushed to the area to strike it rich! As the main stop for people heading north to the gold fields, Seattle boomed with visitors, prospectors, and shoppers.

1907: Pike Place Market opened! The gum wall was years away, but the market was a great place to get food. For more on this awesome place, see page 30.

In the 1890s, the city built a series of wooden pipes to bring in drinking water.

1909: Time to show off a little. Seattle celebrated its 40th anniversary as a city with the Alaska-Yukon-Pacific Exposition. The huge fair showed off what people in the Seattle area built, made, and sold. There were also shows of crafts by the Duwamish and Suquamish people, along with other tribes including the Inuit from Alaska, and Haida and Chinook from Canada.

1916: With World War I underway in Europe, the world needed more ships. Seattle built lots of them! Thousands of people worked in shipyards along Puget Sound.

1930s: The Great Depression caused many people all over America to lose their jobs. Seattle was hit hard, too. Some people there lost their homes, too, and had to live in tents.

1941: The United States entered World War II. This time around, Seattle built airplanes. A lot of the people (about 40 percent!) doing the work were women, because so many men were sent off to fight in the war. This was a big change, especially in this type of factory work. The huge Boeing Company sent planes soaring into the skies around the world.

1941: A dark period in Seattle's history came during World War II. After Japan bombed the U.S. naval base at Pearl Harbor, the government forced all Japanese residents into camps. More than 10,000 people in Seattle were forced into the camps, many losing everything they had.

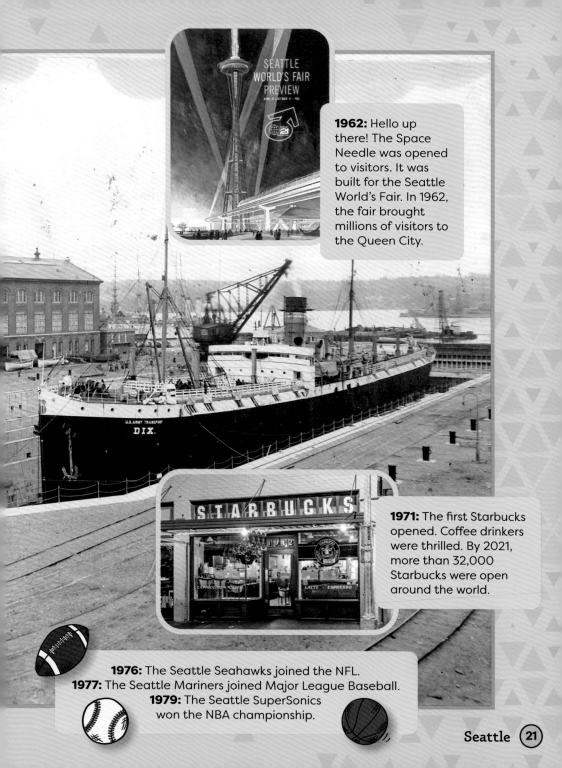

1962: Hello up there! The Space Needle was opened to visitors. It was built for the Seattle World's Fair. In 1962, the fair brought millions of visitors to the Queen City.

1971: The first Starbucks opened. Coffee drinkers were thrilled. By 2021, more than 32,000 Starbucks were open around the world.

1976: The Seattle Seahawks joined the NFL.
1977: The Seattle Mariners joined Major League Baseball.
1979: The Seattle SuperSonics won the NBA championship.

People from the Past!

We could fill a book with amazing people from Seattle history. Here are some folks you might like to meet.

David "Doc" Maynard (1808–1873)

Doc arrived in Seattle in 1852 from Vermont. Within a few years, the energetic guy had become a big part of the young city. He was the first Justice of the Peace, among his many "firsts." He helped lay out the city streets and opened many businesses. Maynard also gets credit for helping change the name of the settlement to honor his friend, Chief Si'ahl of the Duwamish people.

Bertha Knight Landes (1868–1943)

In 1922, she she was one of the first women ever elected to the Seattle City Council. She worked to make safer traffic laws and supported building what became the Seattle Opera House. In 1926, she became the first woman to be elected mayor of a large American city!

FAST FACT

Brian Cladoosby, chairman of the Swinomish tribe from the San Juan Islands, was president of the National Congress of American Indians from 2018 to 2019.

Elmer Knight (1840–1905)

A Scottish architect, his designs helped rebuild Seattle after the Great Fire of 1889. The Pioneer Building still stands today in downtown as an example of his work.

Jacob Furth (1840–1913)

A native of Austria, Furth moved with his family to San Francisco. In 1882, he arrived in Seattle and soon opened what became the city's biggest bank. He was a key city leader after the 1889 fire. He also helped create the city electric, water, and street car companies.

August Wilson (1945–2005)

Wilson was one of the most important playwrights of the 20th century. He wrote about the African American experience, most in the 10 award-winning "Pittsburgh Cycle" plays, including *Fences* and *The Piano Lesson*. He lived in Seattle after 1990 and helped some of his work take the stage at the Seattle Rep Theater.

FAST FACT

The game of Pickleball was invented in Seattle in 1965. It has become a popular "easier" form of tennis.

SEATTLE TODAY

Compared to some other big American cities, Seattle is still pretty young. But it's very busy! Here are some of the things Seattle is best known for today.

Music: The 1960s rock star Jimi Hendrix was from Seattle. In the 1980s and 90s, the music of Pearl Jam and Nirvana established Seattle as the center of grunge, a new style of alternative rock music. Grunge also had its own style, adopted by fans around the world (think flannel shirts and combat boots).

Technology: Big companies like Microsoft, Amazon, and Tableau are based in or near Seattle. Tens of thousands of really smart people work there.

Coffee: Starbucks was just the start. The city has tons of great coffee places. Coffee drinkers look for the newest and coolest drinks everywhere. Why so much coffee? It can get pretty gray and drizzly here, so a warm cuppa in a cozy café became a popular way for folks to get together.

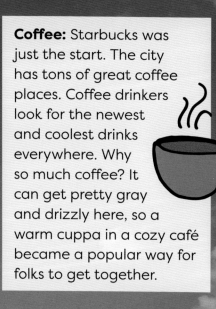

FAST FACT
Seattle is home to more dogs than kids. Really!

Get Outdoors!: Yes, it rains a lot in Seattle. Just wear a raincoat! The city is surrounded by natural beauty in every direction. People from Seattle love to hike, camp, fish, sail, go rock climbing, mountain biking, and much more—and they have a lot of places to enjoy!

SEATTLE for Everyone

Seattle has become a truly diverse, international city. More than 120,000 Asian-Americans or people from Asian countries such as China and Japan live here. Many other Asian nations are also well represented. Since World War II brought workers to airplane factories, a growing Black population has contributed a lot to Seattle's multiculturalism. While they have been denied their native land, Indigenous cultures such as the Suquamish, Duwamish, and Haida continue to impact the land.

Chinatown-International District

People have been coming from China to Seattle since the late 1800s. As in many cities, they built a district where their people lived, and Chinatown has been southeast of Pike Place Market since then. Japanese arrivals set up Japantown, or Nihomachi, near Main Street, north of Chinatown. Other countries and cultures settled there, too. The area became known as the Chinatown-International District.

Little Saigon

In 1965, the United States got rid of a law that limited how many people from Asia could immigrate (that means move in!) to America. Plus, many people were running away from the Vietnam War. For Seattle, that meant people from Vietnam, Cambodia, Laos, and South Korea arrived in larger numbers. Those early arrivals helped create Little Saigon (named for Vietnam's capital), which became part of the International District. One important part of culture is long-standing food traditions that new immigrants brought to share in Seattle. There are many choices from different countries and regions to try!

Indigenous Culture

Seattle and the entire Puget Sound area have been home to indigenous people for more than 10,000 years. Today, members

of the Duwamish, Suquamish, Muckleshoot, Snoqualmie, Tulalip, and Puyallup Nations still live there. The city of Seattle celebrates this history each October 14 on Indigenous Peoples Day. Tourists and locals alike can take part in the Seafair Indian Days Pow Wow in June at Discovery Park. Chief Seattle Days in the fall remember the many contributions of Native people over the years.

Seattle's Black History and Culture

African American settlers first reached the Seattle area before most of the white arrivals. George and Isabella Bush made the long journey west from Missouri in 1845. They made a place to live on Puget Sound in an area still known as Bush Prairie today. In 1861, businessman William Grose built a hotel and restaurant in downtown Seattle. Lumber mills provided some jobs for Black people in the late 1800s.

During World War II, lots of factories making war machines were built near Seattle. The many jobs attracted Black people to the area, mainly moving from the South.

Over time, Black Seattleites settled largely in and around the Central Area, east of downtown. They built businesses, churches, and housing, and their communities flourished, impacting the culture of Seattle. The Civil Rights Movement grew that impact even further with leadership in politics and community organizations making their mark. In recent years, the Black Lives Matter movement saw a lot of support in Seattle from residents from all backgrounds.

40TH YEAR

Festival Sundiata
JUNE 20-21, 2020
SEATTLE CENTER

Since 1980, Seattle's annual Festival Sundiata has celebrated Black culture from around the world.

Scandinavian Influence

In the early 1900s, people from Scandinavian countries who had moved to the U.S. found that Seattle suited them just fine. There were jobs in fishing, lumber, and boat-building—all things they knew how to do from back home. By 1910, about one-third of people in Seattle were Scandinavian.

That heritage remains today. A Nordic Museum (page 50) celebrates this culture. The Ballard Historic District, where many of these Swedes, Norse, Danes, and more lived, remains today the center of Scandinavia in Seattle.

FAST FACTS
There are more people from Iceland living in and around Seattle than any other area in the United States!

Latinx People in Seattle

You can tell Spanish explorers reached the Northwest from the names of some places! The San Juan Islands and the Strait of Juan de Fuca are evidence of their visits in the late 1700s. Though some Mexican immigrants lived and worked on ranches in the early 1900s, it was not until after World War II that a larger number of folks from Central and South America came to Seattle. Then the decades before 2000 saw an even bigger rise in numbers from there. By today, about 10 percent of the people living in Washington state are Latinx. In Seattle, the South Park neighborhood is home to lots of Latinx restaurants and businesses. It's also the site of a popular annual parade called Fiestas Patrias (National Holidays) that celebrates many Latinx cultures.

Why Is It So Doggone Rainy?
Seattle Climate and Weather

Yes, it rains in Seattle. Sometimes, it rains a lot. On average, the area sees some rain on more than 150 days a year. The good part about that rain is that it makes the whole area glow with greenery of all kinds. The bad part is that, well, sometimes you get wet. But it's worth it!

FAST FACTS
Climate means what the weather is like over long periods of time each year. Weather means what it's like outside right now.

Starts in the Jet Stream: The jet stream is a super-fast river of air that swirls around the planet. As it happens, a part of this stream swoops over the Pacific Northwest. Sometimes the jet stream pushes air down toward the ground. This creates weather systems that bring rain to . . . the Pacific Northwest.

Continues from the Pacific: Seattle is not far from the Pacific Ocean, which is, of course, a huge body of water. Some of that water turns into vapor (a gas) and gets pushed by winds toward Seattle.

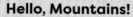

Hello, Mountains!

The vapor smacks into the mountains that surround Seattle. That collects the vapor into clouds that get too heavy to stay up, so . . . down comes the vapor—but after it has turned into (you guessed it!) . . . rain.

It's Not That Bad

It just seems like it rains a lot in Seattle. But it really doesn't. (In some years, New York City gets more total rainfall than Seattle). What makes Seattle seem wetter is that it rains on more days of the year than many other places, but it doesn't rain very much on every one of those days.

When to Visit

July, August, and September are usually very sunny months. Plus, because Seattle is so far north, it is often light until after 9 pm during the summer. Winter is pretty gray—but then again, there are fewer visitors, so it's easier to see what you want to see! It also does not snow that much, perhaps four or five inches a year.

Things to see in Seattle

Tourist time! If you're from Seattle, you (probably) know all about these places. But if you're visiting, here are some of the awesome places you can drag your parents to!

Space Needle

At 520 feet high, this giant tower (at left) is the tallest thing around (well, not as high at Mount Rainier, but the tallest building!). It was built in 1962 as part of the World's Fair. Elevators rocket visitors up, up, and up to a viewing platform (yes, there are windows). You can also eat in a restaurant way up there.

Seattle Center

The Needle is in the middle of the huge Seattle Center. You could spend days just exploring the attractions here! There's a science museum, a glass museum, a children's museum, and even an opera house! Check out page 38 for more details on the museums. Here's the International Fountain spraying high arcs of water!

Pike Place Market

SEATTLE'S TOURIST PLAYGROUND

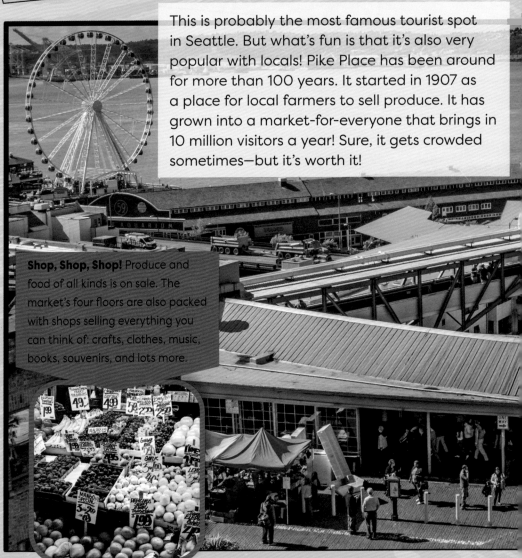

This is probably the most famous tourist spot in Seattle. But what's fun is that it's also very popular with locals! Pike Place has been around for more than 100 years. It started in 1907 as a place for local farmers to sell produce. It has grown into a market-for-everyone that brings in 10 million visitors a year! Sure, it gets crowded sometimes—but it's worth it!

Shop, Shop, Shop! Produce and food of all kinds is on sale. The market's four floors are also packed with shops selling everything you can think of: crafts, clothes, music, books, souvenirs, and lots more.

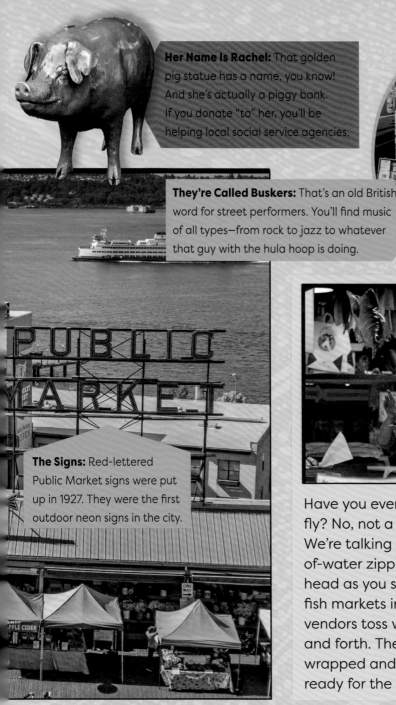

Her Name Is Rachel: That golden pig statue has a name, you know! And she's actually a piggy bank. If you donate "to" her, you'll be helping local social service agencies.

They're Called Buskers: That's an old British word for street performers. You'll find music of all types—from rock to jazz to whatever that guy with the hula hoop is doing.

The Signs: Red-lettered Public Market signs were put up in 1927. They were the first outdoor neon signs in the city.

Have you ever seen a fish fly? No, not a flying fish. We're talking about fish-out-of-water zipping over your head as you shop! At several fish markets in Pike Place, vendors toss whole fish back and forth. Then the fish are wrapped and sold to visitors, ready for the grill or the oven.

Chihuly Garden and Glass

Is that glass or a palm tree? Is that a real seahorse or one made of glass? You'll be blown away (see what I did there? Glass blowing, get it?) by the incredible art in one of Seattle's most famous sites. The creations of artist Dale Chihuly (see box) fill room after room as well as one-of-a-kind garden areas outside. Incredible forms, startling colors, wild shapes—all made with glass! You'll see things here (it's in the Seattle Center) you can't see anywhere else in the world!

Local Hero!

Dale Chihuly was born just down Puget Sound in Tacoma. He studied at U-Dub (see "How to Talk Seattle!") and became a glass artist. After he hurt his arm, Chihuly started working with teams of glassblowers and artists to make his amazing visions come to life. His work can be seen in museums and public spaces all over the world.

Underground Seattle

As you Seattle history fans know (since you already read page 18!), a big fire destroyed a lot of Seattle way back in 1889. To make room for new buildings of fire-safe brick, the old town was mostly buried

Explore underground places like this small workshop.

or covered over. The roads were raised up, too, so what was formerly the ground floor became the basement. It was forgotten for years, but by the 1950s, locals were curious about this underground city. After a little exploring, they found that lots of old buildings, sidewalks, storefronts, and more were still visible—underground! Visitors now can take a walking tour along pathways that were once the heart of Seattle. Head to Pioneer Square to start the tour . . . which happens under your feet!

Burke Museum

History comes alive at this popular spot on the U-Dub campus. See dinosaurs that once walked the region! Explore science with hands-on exhibits! Check out one of the best collections of Native American art from around the Northwest! A series of Chinook sculptures form a walkway into the museum itself.

GET OUT (doors)!

Visitors and locals do have tons of great places to see indoors (not a bad idea on a rainy day). But Seattle is also an outdoor wonderland. You'll find parks all over the city. People here love to be active, so you can play all sorts of sports (page 66). And there are amazing views as you hike around the city and nearby islands (page 86).

With all that water, lots of people enjoy rowing on Lake Washington.

Salmon Ladder

Can fish climb ladders? Salmon can . . . sort of! A canal that lets ships move from Lake Washington into Puget Sound caused some problems for salmon. Those fish needed to go back and forth on the river to reach the place where they lay their eggs. Humans found a solution! A series of concrete pools was built alongside the canal locks (where ships pass through). The salmon leap from pool to pool (right) to "climb" back up the flowing river. It's a popular spot for tourists to watch the leaping fishies!

Gas Works Park was built on the former site of a huge factory. Some of the old buildings were left as decorations!

GETTING AROUND
SEATTLE

Buses, cars, bikes, sure, Seattle has all of that. But it has something most cities don't have. Seattle has a monorail! That's a train that runs on a single cement track. The monorail was built for the World's Fair. The track is only a mile long, and is one of only a few working monorails in the U.S.

Bikes: The Burke-Gilman Trail is just one of several bike paths in Seattle. You can pedal in green lanes near Green Lake, Lake Union, or the Ship Canal, among other places. Wear your helmet—it's the law!

Water Taxi: Seattle has so much water around it, you can be sure there are boats. In fact, Washington state boasts the largest ferry system in the U.S., with twenty-one ferries that carry 24 million people around Puget Sound and the greater Salish Sea each year. (The Salish Sea separates Washington state and Canada). Ferries carry people to nearby Bainbridge and Vashon islands and cities on the Kitsap peninsula. There are also water taxis to splash from place to place. More fun than a car!

Streetcars: The city used to have lots of these vehicles—starting in 1884 with horse-drawn streetcars—but most closed down years ago (the electric streetcar system closed in 1941). However, one line was brought back in 2007, and another opened in 2016. Take a fun ride on the South Lake Union or First Hill lines!

IT'S OFFICIAL!

Cities like to name "official" things. That basically just means that lots of people who live there like something! Here are some of Seattle's "official" city things.

OFFICIAL
CITY BIRD:
Great Blue Heron

CITY OF GOODWILL • SEATTLE

OFFICIAL CITY FLAG:
Seattle added "City of Goodwill" in 1990. That year it hosted a big sports event called the Goodwill Games.

OFFICIAL WASHINGTON STATE STUFF
Bird: willow goldfinch
Amphibian: Pacific chorus frog
Fish: Steelhead trout
Marine mammal: Orca (killer whale)
Local animal: Olympic marmot

OFFICIAL CITY FLOWER:
Dahlia

OFFICIAL CITY SONG:

"Seattle the Peerless City"

Peerless means better
than anything else!

Fremont Troll: The Fremont Troll stands 18 feet high and weighs more than 13,000 pounds!

Art in Seattle

Yes, that's a giant troll statue living under a bridge. He's in the Fremont district. Four local artists made this famous troll in 1990.

The troll is not the only public art in Seattle (see below). For art that you can enjoy indoors, turn the page for more details of more details.

Chihully Garden and Glass. p. 36

Outdoor Art

People in Seattle love being outdoors. Artists have created lots of fun things for those busy hikers and bikers to check out.

Too Big to Eat: A huge double popsicle leans over visitors to Belltown's neighborhood.

The Wall of Death: A sculpture on the Burke-Gilman bike trail is not as dangerous as its name!

Black Sun: Peer through the center and spot the Space Needle far away! This piece by Isamu Noguchi is in Volunteer Park.

Forever Waiting: This statue shows a group of people waiting for a streetcar in Fremont. So far, it has not arrived!

Art in Seattle

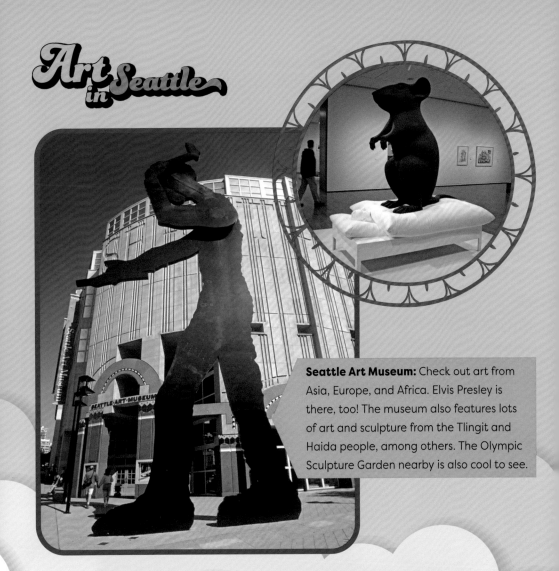

Seattle Art Museum: Check out art from Asia, Europe, and Africa. Elvis Presley is there, too! The museum also features lots of art and sculpture from the Tlingit and Haida people, among others. The Olympic Sculpture Garden nearby is also cool to see.

Frye Art Museum: Charles and Henry Frye made a lot of money in business in Seattle. They also bought a lot of art! In 1952, the family gave all the art to the city to display in this museum. Lots of paintings and other art has been added since. Today, it's a great mix of classic styles and modern artists.

Seattle Asian Art: Art that is new and modern: art that is centuries old. You'll find it all in this big museum. All the art is from countries in Asia, where more than 120,000 people in Seattle are from. See sculptures, paintings, ceramics, and much more. It's like visiting dozens of countries all in one building!

OBAMA: No, not the former president. This is one of Seattle's oddest museums. The Official Bad Art Museum (get it?) includes, well . . . just what it says. It might be trash, but here at OBAMA—it's art!

Henry Art Gallery: It's no surprise that the art on display at the University of Washington is young and new. After all, so are most of the students! The Henry has the coolest and newest modern art on display. Exhibitions change often—so go more than once!

Other Great Seattle Museums

Museums are great for more than art, of course. Seattle has something for just about everyone!

Pacific Science Center: Shoot a water cannon, wander through a butterfly forest, see how your body grows, and try the daring high-wire ride! This scien-fantastic place is fun . . . and good for your brain!

Museum of Pop Culture: Paul Allen helped create Microsoft in Seattle. That earned him a LOT of money. He used some of it to help build this awesome place to visit, inspired by his love of rock music, science fiction, and pop culture (which is pretty much anything that people have fun with). Listen to music, see cool films, and check out the great displays of new (and not so new) stuff.

Wooden Boat Museum: Boats made Seattle what it is today. This cool place shows off the history of the watercraft from canoes to large sailing ships. On Sundays, you can take a trip on one of them.

Museum of Flight: If you like aircraft, this is heaven. This museum is south of Seattle near the Boeing Company site. Hundreds of flying things of all sizes fill one of the largest buildings in the world. See everything from an early biplane to the supersonic Concorde to an Air Force One that carried U.S. presidents.

Museum of History and Industry: Celebrate Seattle history and its contributions to the world here. Displays take you back in local history, show off some of the inventions from Seattle, and let you see the world through a periscope!

Seattle Children's Museum: Hands-on fun for little kids! Explore a village, help run the market, and be a builder! You'll find it in the Seattle Center's Armory building.*

Rubber Chicken Museum?: Yes, there is one. Well, it's more of a large display case inside a wacky store in Seattle. But it still has rubber chicken history, rubber chicken models, rubber chicken gear. Clucky you!

*Scheduled to re-open in 2022.

See the World in Seattle

People have come to Seattle from around the world. Their cultures, lives, and impact on the area are celebrated at these places.

▼ **Duwamish Longhouse and Cultural Center** For thousands of years, Duwamish people lived in the area. They often built longhouses, wooden buildings that could fit many people. A modern version is now a small museum. Visit and imagine what life was like hundreds of years ago!

National Nordic Museum ▶
Take a trip to Scandinavia in the Ballard neighborhood. Celebrate Viking heritage and see artifacts from Sweden, Denmark, Finland, Norway, and Iceland.

Northwest African American Museum ▼
NAAM features the visual arts, music, crafts, literature, and history of African Americans in the Northwest. It focuses on people whose journeys began in slavery as well as recent immigrants from places such as Somalia, Sudan, and Ethiopia.

◀ **Wing Luke Museum of the Asian Pacific Experience**
This museum connects visitors to the dynamic history, cultures, and art of Asian Pacific Americans through amazing storytelling and inspiring experiences.

Performing Arts

While rock music is Seattle's most famous type of performance, there are more than seventy clubs where you (or probably your grown-ups) can hear music every night. Meanwhile, other artists show off their skills all over the area.

Singers! The Seattle Opera is one of the leading opera companies in the U.S. They have a Youth Opera Project for kids who love the history and drama of opera.

Dancers! Check out the Pacific Northwest Ballet.

Benaroya Hall is home to the Seattle Symphony, which brings people together and lifts the human spirit.

See plays of all kinds at Seattle Rep, ACT, 5th Avenue Theater and other venues.

How to Talk Seattle

Just about every place in the world has some words that only make sense to locals. Here are a few examples of "only in Seattle" words or phrases.

"THE MOUNTAIN IS OUT."

Say this when the weather is clear enough to see nearby Mount Rainier and other peaks.

SEATTLE TUXEDO

A plaid flannel shirt. A real tuxedo is a fancy dark suit worn with a bowtie. Folks in Seattle are pretty easygoing. Dressing like a lumberjack is just fine for any event!

U-Dub

University of Washington
("double-u," get it?)

Liquid Sunshine

That is: Rain!
Yes, it rains a
lot in Seattle.
But everyone there
doesn't seem
to mind!

Pill Hill

The neighborhood with most of
the hospitals and doctors' offices.
Pills . . . doctors . . . get it?

SEATTLE: It's Weird!

Gum Wall

Near Pike Place Market is the grossest wall in the world. For years, people have stuck their chewed-up gum to the wall. Yes. Sticky, icky, germy, chewed-up gum. To the wall. A LOT! It's really gross and has its picture taken more than the Space Needle, probably.

WORLD FAMOUS
GIANT SHOE MUSEUM

WORLD'S LARGEST COLLECTION OF GIANT SHOES

Greatest Shoe

See a SHOE Actually worn by WORLD'S TALLEST MAN

SEATTLE'S SHOES OF MYSTERY

Sure, Why Not?

Visit the Giant Shoe Museum, only in Seattle! It's not a giant museum, it's all about really, really big shoes!

Those Are BIG Boots!

Speaking of big shoes, in Oxbow Park, Paul Bunyan must have dropped his 22-foot-tall boots. There is also an enormous red cowboy hat that is 44 feet across!

Don't Tilt!

Pinball was the way kids played video games long ago. Of course, they still make new pinball machines, too. And you can see (and play!) more than 60 games at the Pinball Museum. Because . . . why not?

Hey! I'm from Seattle too!

Bill Gates

Born in Seattle: October 28, 1955

Gates founded Microsoft in Seattle. It was one of the world's first and biggest tech companies. He is one of the richest people in the world! He left Microsoft in 2020. Today, he uses his wealth to help millions of people around the world.

Gail Devers

Born in Seattle: November 19, 1966
Gail is one of the most successful female track and field athletes in U.S. history! She was the second woman ever to win back-to-back Olympic gold medals in the 100-meter race (1992 and 1996). She was also a world champion three times!

What People Do
IN SEATTLE

More than 700,000 people live in Seattle itself. But that jumps to nearly four million people if you include nearby cities and towns around the Sound. Here are some of the most popular ways that people make a living in this area.

Amazon is huge. Really, really huge. And it started here, so more than 75,000 Amazonians still work in Seattle. The company's headquarters is in the Denny Triangle area.

The other big Seattle original is microsoft. most of its 57,000 workers are based in Redmond, which is a suburb to the east of downtown Seattle.

millions of people come to Seattle to have fun . . . and tens of thousands of local folks work to make that happen. Hotels, restaurants, tour guides, and attractions employ folks of all ages all over the area.

Biotechnology combines computers and tech with humans and animals. Thanks to the scientific folks at the many universities and colleges, many companies here find ways to help people get healthy.

How do all those fish get to all those plates? Fisherfolk! Fishing is a big industry that sends boats and ships into the sound and into the Pacific to bring back seafood of all sorts. Popular items include salmon, oysters, crab, and clams.

Look! Up in the sky! It's something built in Seattle! Well, nearby, anyway. The Boeing Company is one of the biggest aircraft makers in the world. More than 70,000 Boeing-ers work in Washington to make some of the biggest planes in the world.

Eat the Seattle Way

If you love seafood, you'll LOVE Seattle. Fresh food from the water can be found in lots of restaurants and stores—from salmon, trout, and bass to crabs, clams, and oysters. But that's not the only type of food that people in Seattle enjoy.

People in Seattle put cream cheese on their hot dogs. What?! Really.

Jones Soda Co. Can you drink turkey, bubble gum, and fufu berry (whatever that is!)? Thanks to Jones Soda Company, you can. Along with "usual" flavors like cream, root beer, and cola, this Seattle company does a Thanksgiving Special set, along with other new and unusual flavors. A sip of Birthday Cake, anyone?

Eat It . . . Or Run Away From It?
It looks like a sea monster, but it's really a kind of clam. It is spelled geoduck, but you call it "gooey-duck." And people actually eat these things!

Bubble Tea

Bubble Tea That's what Seattleites call tea with boba, the little gooey, chewy balls of tapioca. It's super-popular in Seattle. Some places specialize in it, while others just have it on the menu for fans. Check out the super-wide straws some folks use to slurp their boba!

What We Eat From Washington
Apples * Cherries * Salmon
Potatoes * Apricots

Salmon 100 Ways

Five types of Pacific salmon are served all over Seattle. People grill it, steam it, roast it, bake it, and sushi it (well, you know . . . make it into sushi). Most of it is caught in nearby waters, so you know it's fresh, fresh, fresh!

FAST FACT
Science stuff! Oysters are a type of animal called a bivalve mollusk!

Everybody Eats Oysters!

Oysters have long been a huge part of the diet of people around Seattle. The Duwamish and Suquamish people ate them by the tens of thousands. Enormous mounds of empty oyster shells have been found at ancient sites. When the weather turns cold, that's when oysters can be harvested safely. People seek them out in the many bodies of water around Puget Sound. (You can also find them at restaurants, of course!)

World's Best Mac and Cheese

Beecher's restaurant serves this dish. Why World's Best? Well, because they say so. Check it out and let them know if they're right!

Go, Seattle Sports!

Seattle is home to some awesome pro sports teams. Go, team, go!

Russell Wilson

SEATTLE SEAHAWKS

Joined the National Football League in 1976.

Won Super Bowl XLVIII; also played in Super Bowls after the 2005 and 2014 seasons.

Famous for having the 12th Man, fans who are so loud they freak out the opposition!

Big Names: Steve Largent, Kenny Easley, Marshawn Lynch, Russell Wilson

Home: Lumen Field

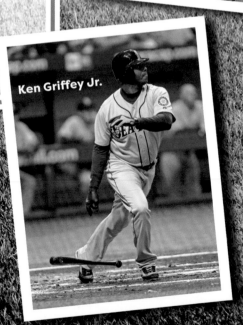

Kyle Seager

SEATTLE MARINERS

Joined Major League Baseball in 1976.

Haven't made the World Series yet, but have reached the playoffs four times.

Big Names: Ken Griffey Jr., Edgar Martinez, Randy Johnson, Ichiro Suzuki, Felix Hernandez

Home: T-Mobile Park

Ken Griffey Jr.

Seattle used to be home to the NBA's SuperSonics. They won the NBA championship in 1979. In 2008, the team moved to Oklahoma City and became the Thunder.

Sue Bird

SEATTLE STORM

Joined the WNBA in 2000.

Have won four league championships: 2004, 2010, 2018, 2020!

They are one of only two teams with four titles.

Big Names: Sue Bird, Swin Cash, Breanna Stewart

Home: Alaska Airlines Arena

In 1917, the Seattle Metropolitans were the first team from the United States to win the Stanley Cup as champions of pro hockey.

SEATTLE KRAKEN

Joined National Hockey League in 2021.

Yes, they were named for a sea monster!

Team says home arena will be first carbon-neutral sports palace ever!

Big Names: We'll see!

Home: Climate Pledge Arena

SEATTLE SOUNDERS

Joined Major League Soccer in 2009.

One of the most successful teams of the 2010s—have never missed MLS playoffs.

Won MLS Cup in 2016 and 2019.

Has super-loyal fans; team held MLS attendance record for many years.

Big Names: Clint Dempsey, Fredy Montero, Stefan Frei

Home: Lumen Field

Other Sports!

It's not just watching . . . it's playing! People in Seattle are super active. Here are some of the ways they get out and sweat!

For great **skiing and snowboarding**, check out Snoqualamie Pass, Stevens Pass, Crystal Mountain or other areas, most within a couple of hours of downtown!

All that water is so inviting. So get out on it! **Sea kayaking** and **rowing** are very popular on the lakes and rivers of Seattle. Lots of places rent you all the gear you'll need.

Fore! Most of the best **golf courses** are scattered around the edges of Seattle. But nearly all of them have amazing views, so it won't matter how many of your shots end up in the water!

All around Seattle are rocks. So it's no surprise that **rock climbing** is a very popular sport. Routes range from easy bouldering to super-challenging. Don't do this alone, of course, but get an adult and try it out together!

Who needs a car? **Hiking** is probably Seattle's favorite pastime. Trails can be found in city parks and in just about every direction from the Space Needle to the mountains! Find a trail guide and choose a hike that's right for your family.

There are hundreds of miles of trails made for **bicycles** in and around Seattle. The Burke-Gilman is the most popular, but you can find places to pedal near U-Dub, in West Seattle, around Lake Union, and more.

COLLEGE TOWN

While one university is the biggest game in town, it's not the only place to college! Here's where you can study someday!

UNIVERSITY OF WASHINGTON

Founded 1861
Students: 46,000
Popular majors: biomedicine, social science; engineering; computer science
Fast Fact: The Huskies sports teams play in the Pac-12, one of the biggest college sports conferences.

SEATTLE UNIVERSITY

Founded 1891
Students: 4,500
Popular majors: business, engineering, biomedicine
Fast Fact: Right in the heart of town, Seattle U. is a Catholic school run by the order known as the Jesuits.

SEATTLE PACIFIC UNIVERSITY

Founded 1891
Students: 2,500
Popular majors: business, engineering, social science
Fast Fact: SPU is a Christian university, founded by the Methodists.

UNIVERSITY OF PUGET SOUND

Founded 1888
Students: 2,300
Popular majors: business, psychology, visual arts
Fast Fact: Located near Tacoma, UPS is often on lists of most beautiful college campuses.

CORNISH COLLEGE OF THE ARTS

Founded 1914
Students: 650
Popular majors: performing and visual arts
Fast Fact: Cornish also offers lots of art classes that can be taken by the public.

LOL!
Seattle Sillies

Go ahead and laugh at Seattle—its people won't mind! Here are some riddles to tickle your funny bone.

How do astronauts get vaccinated?

With the Space Needle!

Which Star Wars character left the most gum on the gum wall?

Chewbacca!

Which state does the most laundry?

Wash-ington!

What do pirates use for money at the University of Washington?

U-Dubloons!

Which magical creatures carry Seattleites over the water?

Ferries!

What's the wettest mountain?

Mount Rainier!

What do they call the flying salmon at the Pike Place Market?

The catch of the day!

It's Alive! Animals in Seattle

Seattle's natural world is packed with places for animals to live. They find homes in the water, in forests, in parks and open spaces, and even in some neighborhoods! And don't forget to look up to spot flying animals (and not just birds!).

Woodpeckers

Tidepools
(Discovery Park)

Black-tailed
deer

River otters

Anna's hummingbird

Beavers

Northwest Trek Wildlife Park

A couple of hours south of Seattle is a very wild place—really! Hundreds of animals roam around a huge open space. In your car (or on a tour), you get right up close to bison, wolves, moose, elk, and other animals native to the Northwest United States. Other areas are home to wild cats, bears, and lots of amazing birds.

It's Alive! Animals in Seattle

Seattle and the water go together like peanut butter and jelly. The waters around the city are packed with amazing sea life. You can see some of them on tours that leave from the waterfront. But sometimes you just need sharp eyes from the shore!

Rockfish

Orca

Tufted puffin

Humpback whales

Osprey

Sea lion

They're Not Killer Whales!

Orcas used to be called that nasty name. Today, we know better! They are actually a big member of the dolphin family and not really whales. No matter what family they are in, they are fast and fierce. Orcas live by the dozens in pods around Puget Sound and other waterways.

WE SAW IT AT THE ZOO

Penguins and jaguars and gorillas, oh my! Since 1899, the Woodland Park Zoo has been the place for Seattleites to see awesome animals. Part of the zoo is on land that was created by Guy Phinney, a rich English dude, for his deer park. The zoo grew from there, adding a children's zoo in 1967. More than a million people head to Green Lake to see the animals in person.

Some of the highlights include a butterfly garden, a special Northwest trail to meet "local" animals, and trips to Asia, Africa, and a rain forest. The Humboldt penguins are one of the most popular exhibits. Say hi for us!

Sumatran tiger

Bontebok

Patas monkey

A Walking Watermelon

In 2020, Ulan the tapir had a baby daughter. After seeing her stripes, zoo folks nicknamed the baby Watermelon. She has become a big hit with visitors and her birthday on June 10 is always a big day. Tapirs look a bit like pigs with longer noses, but they're really related to horses. Tapirs live mostly in South America (and, of course, Seattle!).

A baby tapir

Meerkat

WOODLAND PARK ZOO

Seattle Aquarium

Check out swimmers at this Seattle Center site. Local heroes like seals and sea lions are featured, along with hands-on tidepool animals. The biggest exhibit is the Underwater Dome. Don't worry—you won't get wet! Stand in the dome and pretend you're underwater as you watch tons of fish swim by.

One Big Park!

Discovery Park

The highlight of the Seattle park system is this enormous wonderland. It covers a huge area of the peninsula (there's that word again!) on the north of Elliott Bay (the part of Puget Sound that touches Seattle's waterfront). Most of the park has incredible views of the water. Hiking trails let you follow the shoreline or explore the forested part of the park.

A big highlight are the tidepools that can be found where the water meets the land (check the tides for best times!). Sharp-eyed explorers will find crabs, urchins, lobsters, fish, and other creatures!

Make sure to take a short walk to the Discovery Park Lighthouse at West Point. Still an active beacon, it was first lit in 1881!

Spooky Sights

Do you believe in ghosts and spirits? Not everyone does . . . but no one knows for sure! Like most cities, Seattle has lots of places that people say are haunted.

Does the **Moore Theatre** host a ghost? Some people say that James Moore, who founded the giant movie palace in 1909, can be seen and heard drifting through the seats!

Is that a ghost in the mirror? People who have eaten at **Kells Irish restaurant** say they have seen a little girl popping up in the glass . . . to watch you while you eat! Another ghost named Charlie tips his derby hat to say hi. Aaaahhh! Some people say this is one of the most haunted buildings in America!

Is this hotel too spooky to check into? The **Sorrento Hotel** has gotten national attention for its many sightings. Writer Alice B. Toklas went to school at the University of Washington in the 1890s. She died in 1967. Visitors to room 408 report seeing her wispy form drifting around!

Are you freaked by Frank? A ghost by that name has been seen lurking near the **Pike Place Market**.

Is that a spirit in the hallway? If you go to school at **West Seattle High**, rumor has it that you won't be alone . . . students from the past loved school so much—they stuck around spookily!

Festivals!

Time to celebrate! Along with the usual holidays that most places enjoy, Seattle has some of its own special events. Visitors and locals alike enjoy getting out and having fun!

Fremont Solstice Parade: Celebrate the longest day of the year each summer in this neighborhood north of downtown. Giant puppets, funky music, colorful costumes, and an arts-and-crafts fair are all part of this creative salute to the solstice.

Chief Seattle Days: On Bainbridge Island, this event has been happening since 1911. The Suquamish people present art, dance, music, and crafts. Check out the salmon bake and watch a canoe race. The event is usually in late August.

Dragonfest: Lions and dragons dance and martial artists flip and twirl. Korean and Japanese drums sound their call, and Chinatown's streets fill with the smell of amazing food. There is even hula dancing and a noodle-eating contest. The celebration has been happening each summer for more than 40 years.

Seafair: With water events galore, this annual salute to boating (among other things) draws thousands of people to Genesee Park. High-speed boats race offshore, and the Blue Angels Air Force jets often zoom overhead. Between races, concerts and tons of food are ready to tempt visitors. Seafair started in 1951 to honor Seattle's 100th birthday!

Northwest Folklife: Memorial Day weekend draws music lovers to Seattle Center for this celebration of folk tunes. Local musicians of all sorts present traditional and original music. There are also lots of displays by local artists and craftspeople.

Christmas Ship Festival: Santa comes on a boat in Seattle! The Christmas Ship travels around Puget Sound during the holiday season, bright lights blinking. It makes stops at different waterfronts where people can come on board to meet Santa and enjoy holiday music. The cool part is that dozens (or hundreds) of smaller boats deck out their decks with holiday lights for a floating parade.

SEATTLE BY THE NUMBERS

Stats and facts and digits galore! Here are some of the numbers that make Seattle what it is.

COFFEE GRANDE!

In 2020, WalletHub.com scored Seattle No. 1 in the United States as the city that is best for coffee lovers!

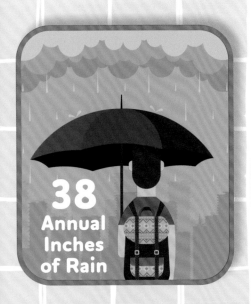

38 Annual Inches of Rain

$63 MILLION!

Cost to Build Bill Gates' Big House

905 *feet*
Deepest Part of Puget Sound

2
Rank of Seattle among world cities in number of glassblowing studios

147 freshwater
53 saltwater
Miles of Shoreline

World Record!
The Evergreen Point Floating Bridge is the longest one of those in the world! It stretches 15,580 feet between Bellevue and Seattle.

1
Rank of Seattle among U.S. cities in digital downloads of library books

21,000,000*
Annual Visitors
*And growing!

A Seattle First: In 1987, the city became the first in the U.S. to send out police officers on mountain bikes. The idea has spread to places all over America.

Not Far Away

Whether you live in Seattle or you're just visiting the city, don't forget that many other awesome places to visit are very close by. Get a driver and hit the road for these fun day (or so!) trips.

What a view! The long drive to **Olympic National Park** was worth it!

Wow! Could you see the Pacific?

Yup. We drove to the top of Hurricane Ridge and saw the ocean on one side and the mountains on the other. We also hiked a rain forest and saw lots of animals.

😮 Jealous!

It was worth the drive. This place has so much to see and do; lots of different environments all in one national park!

Splash! Just left **Snoqualmie Falls**!

Where is it?

Just off the road east of Seattle. It was so LOUD!

How close can you get?

There are walkways at the bottom and near the top; we even got a little wet from the spray!

Whew! Made it to the top of **Mount Rainier**! Yay!

FAST FACT
Mount Rainier can be seen from downtown Seattle on clear days. It's the fifth-tallest U.S. mountain at 14,411 feet.

How long did it take?

About two hours to drive here . . . took a whole long day to hike up! Tired!

You're brave! Can I try it?

Well, you have to be in good shape and hike at the right time of year (summer is best).

Awesome! I'll get out my hiking shoes!

We took the ferry to **Bainbridge Island**! We saw orcas on the way there. It was only about a half hour!

Cool! What did you do on the island?

Great hikes, cute inns, super views of the city.

Did you know **Tacoma** means "source of the waters"?

Dude! That's cool!

Yeah, that's from the Salish language. That's what the original people here called Mount Rainier!

Did not know that!

But Tacoma is also a pretty big city south of Seattle. It has a great glass museum and some great parks on Puget Sound.

Let's go!

We needed our car AND a ferry to reach **San Juan Island**.

Worth the trip?

Totally! This place is beautiful, full of forests and great hiking paths.

Cold?

No, not really. And there are other islands up here to explore. Great views!

A Whole 'Nother Country, Eh?

There is another giant nation just 120 miles north of Seattle. Hello, Canada! It's a huge country, but there are some Canadian attractions that are Seattle-close.

Victoria: Visiting this beautiful Canadian city is like taking a trip to England. You'll even see the double-decker buses like they have in London! There are beautiful gardens to visit and lots of great food from around the world. Take a fast ferry ride north from Seattle to reach the island home of Victoria (bring your passport!).

Peace Arch: You can have a foot in two countries at this site in Surrey, British Columbia (or from the U.S. side). A stone arch in a beautiful park crosses the international border.

Vancouver: This is the biggest city in western Canada and it's only about two hours north of Seattle by car. Like Seattleites, people in Vancouver love to get outdoors! Stanley Park is one of the best city parks in the country, packed with hiking, biking, lakes, and more. Vancouver is on the water, too, so there is sailing, whale watching, and fishing. The city has a big Asian population, so look for some tasty dishes from China and other places.

Sister Cities Around the World

Did you know cities can have sisters? Why not brothers? Well, that's just what they're called. Sister Cities was started in 1956 as a program of the U.S. government. The idea was to connect cities here and around the world to help people get to know each other. This was not long after World War II, so making new friends was pretty important! Seattle jumped on board quickly and today is a Sister City to 20 cities around the world.

Reykjavik, Iceland

Bergen, Norway

Galway, Ireland

Gdynia, Poland

Nantes, France

Pécs, Hungary

Perugia, Italy

Tashkent, Uzbekistan

Daejeon, Korea

Kobe, Japan

Be'er Sheva, Israel

Chongqing, China

Kaohsiung, Taiwan

Haiphong, Vietnam

Sihanoukville, Cambodia

Cebu, Philippines

Limbe, Cameroon

Mombasa, Kenya

Surabaya, Indonesia

Christchurch, New Zealand

Seattle's Sister Cities

Sister Cities in Action

Here are some examples of how Seattle is working with and helping its sister cities:

Mombasa: Seattle residents help support a group in Kenya that gives jobs to local people making products from coconut oil. Seattle also helps support an orphanage in the city.

Tashkent: This was the first Sister City in what was then the Soviet Union. There is a Seattle Peace Park in Tashkent designed by both U.S. and Uzbeki people. Folk dancers have visited each other's city to perform as well.

Chongqing: The zoos in these two cities share information and animals, while a pair of high schools has teamed up for a long time to connect students. A group of Seattleites worked with this Sister City group to make the Seattle Chinese Garden in Chongqing.

Reykjavik: More Icelanders live in Seattle than in any other U.S. city! Exchanges between the two cities have included music, arts, and students. The sister city program hosts two artists from Iceland to study each year in Seattle.

FIND OUT MORE!

Books, Websites, and More!

Books

Coleman, Ted. *Seattle Seahawks Superstars.* North Star Editions, 2021.

Connery-Boyd, Peg. *Totally Pacific Northwest: The Big Book of Activities.* Hawk's Nest, 2016.

Gaydos, Joseph K. *Explore the Salish Sea? A Nature Guide for Kids.* Bigfoot Press, 2018.

Levy, Janey. *Native Peoples of the Northwest Coast.* Gareth Stevens, 2016.

Olympic National Park Activity Book. Little Bison Press, 2021.

Smith, Roland. *E Is for Evergreen. A Washington State Alphabet.* Sleeping Bear Press, 2010.

Williams, David B. *Seattle Walks: Discovering History and Nature in the City.* University of Washington Press, 2017.

Web Sites

https://www.seattleschild.com
Activity guide for kids of all ages.

https://visitseattle.org/things-to-do/families/
The official Visit Seattle site pages for family activities.

https://familydestinationsguide.com/fun-things-to-do-seattle-kids
Another place for families to find things to do in Seattle!

https://thechildrensmuseum.org
Inside one of the country's biggest kids' museums.

Photo Credits and Thanks

Photos from Dreamstime, Shutterstock, or Wikimedia unless noted.

Flickr: Coetzee 51; Ruth Hartnup, 54B. Focus on Sports: 62L, 63BR. National Archives: 20C. Newscom: Gary Bogdon/KRT 57; Nick Wosika/ Icon Sportswire 64L. NOAA: 30B. Seattle Municipal Archives: 14C, 16T, 16L, 16C, 18C, 63T. Visit Seattle: 10, 14L, 34C, 38, 39B, 47B, 48-49-50 (all), 66B, 67B, 77R, 78.

Artwork: Shutterstock: Spreadthesign 8L; LemonadePixel 24B, 31TB, 42B, 58-59; danceyourlife 43B, 51. Maps (6-7): Jessica Nevins.

Cultural Content Consultant: Jennifer E. Ellwood.

Thanks to our pal Nancy Ellwood and the fine folks at Arcadia!

INDEX

Thanks for Visiting

SEATTLE

Come Back Soon!